PRAISE FOR
THE ROAD TO LEADERSHIP

"The Road to Leadership *is an absolutely delightful, informative, and engaging book. Huston provides clear, honest, valuable leadership lessons—combined with quotes and personal stories—to help readers appreciate that leadership development is a shared journey and realize that all nurses can and must be leaders. I encourage anyone with the passion to make the world a better place for patients, providers, and the nursing profession to read and be guided by this book."*

–Theresa M. "Terry" Valiga, EdD, RN, CNE, ANEF, FAAN
Professor Emerita, Duke University School of Nursing

"The phrase 'art and science' is often used when describing aspects of the nursing profession. The fact is, nurses are educated in the science of nursing, including nursing leadership. It is only through practice, experience, and mentorship that nurses develop the art of nursing. This text by a proven nurse leader provides actionable guidance for nurses desiring to develop and grow the art of nursing leadership. Thank you, Carol, for candidly sharing your insights so that others may benefit from your leadership journey."

–Kenneth W. Dion, PhD, RN, MSN, MBA
...se entrepreneur, inventor, consultant, educator, and lecturer
...rer, Honor Society of Nursing, Sigma Theta Tau International

"Dr. Huston makes a compelling case that leadership should not be learned through trial and error with costly consequences but through knowledge, intention, and awareness of self and the environment. With extraordinary wisdom and reflection, she reminds us of a moral imperative that 'all nurses can and must be leaders.' Her insight about leadership bears witness to these lessons through her personal exemplars from clinical practice, education, and professional membership associations. In The Road to Leadership, Dr. Huston shares her legacy and leadership journey—sometimes painful but always authentic. This book is a must-read for those who aspire to lead or those who have been inspired."

–Donna M. Nickitas, PhD, RN, NEA-BC, CNE, FNAP, FAAN
Professor, Hunter Bellevue School of Nursing
Executive Officer, Nursing Science PhD Program
The Graduate Center, City University of New York

"I'm not surprised that Carol Huston has synthesized her leadership into these nine seminal principles. She has demonstrated these principles in her own life and leadership, and it has paid off in the quality of her relationships and her impact on friends, colleagues, students, and community. If we simply focus on these principles, we cannot help but transform our lives, our relationships, and those we serve. Thanks for these nine key values, Carol, and for being their best ambassador in your own life and leadership."

–Tim Porter-O'Grady, DM, EdD, ScD(h), APRN, FAAN, FACCWS
Senior Partner, Health Systems, Tim Porter-O'Grady Associates Inc., Atlanta, Georgia.
Clinical Professor, Leadership Scholar, The Ohio State University College of Nursing, Columbus, Ohio
Professor, School of Nursing; Deans Advisory Board, Emory University, Atlanta, Georgia
Chair of the Board, American Nurses Foundation

"Carol Huston hit the mark with her use of personal lessons learned to offer advice to new nurse leaders. Her down-to-earth ideas are clear and effective tools for nurses to follow on the path to effective leadership. The mix of narrative chapter information and thought-provoking quotes adds pleasure to the reader's experience."

–Karen M. Estridge, DNP, RN
Assistant Professor, College of Nursing and Health Sciences
Ashland University

THE ROAD TO LEADERSHIP

CAROL J. HUSTON,
DPA, MSN, RN, FAAN

Sigma Theta Tau International
Honor Society of Nursing®

The Honor Society of Nursing, Sigma Theta Tau International (STTI) is a nonprofit organization whose mission is advancing world health and celebrating nursing excellence in scholarship, leadership, and service. Founded in 1922, STTI has more than 135,000 active members in over 90 countries and territories. Members include practicing nurses, instructors, researchers, policymakers, entrepreneurs, and others. STTI's 530 chapters are located at more than 700 institutions of higher education throughout Armenia, Australia, Botswana, Brazil, Canada, Colombia, England, Ghana, Hong Kong, Japan, Jordan, Kenya, Lebanon, Malawi, Mexico, the Netherlands, Pakistan, Philippines, Portugal, Singapore, South Africa, South Korea, Swaziland, Sweden, Taiwan, Tanzania, Thailand, the United States, and Wales. Learn more at www.nursingsociety.org.

Sigma Theta Tau International
550 West North Street
Indianapolis, IN, USA 46202

To order additional books, buy in bulk, or order for corporate use, contact Nursing Knowledge International at 888.NKI.4YOU (888.654.4968/US and Canada) or +1.317.634.8171 (outside US and Canada).

To request a review copy for course adoption, email solutions@nursingknowledge.org or call 888.NKI.4YOU (888.654.4968/US and Canada) or +1.317.634.8171 (outside US and Canada).

To request author information, or for speaker or other media requests, contact Marketing, Honor Society of Nursing, Sigma Theta Tau International at 888.634.7575 (US and Canada) or +1.317.634.8171 (outside US and Canada).

ISBN: 9781945157608
ISBN epub: 9781945157806
ISBN PDF: 9781945157622
ISBN Mobi: 9781945157813

Library of Congress Cataloging-in-Publication data

Names: Huston, Carol Jorgensen, author.

Title: The Road to Leadership / Carol
  J. Huston.

Description: Indianapolis, IN : Sigma Theta Tau International, 2018. |
  Includes bibliographical references.

Identifiers: LCCN 2017037009| ISBN 9781945157608 (print : alk. paper) | ISBN
  9781945157622 (pdf)

Subjects: | MESH: Leadership | Nursing | Attitude | Nurses' Instruction

Classification: LCC RT82 | NLM WY 105 | DDC 610.7306/9--dc23 LC record available at
https://lccn.loc.gov/2017037009

First Printing, 2017

Publisher: Dustin Sullivan

Acquisitions Editor: Emily Hatch

Editorial Coordinator: Paula Jeffers

Cover Designer: Rebecca Batchelor

Interior Design/Page Layout: Rebecca Batchelor

Principal Book Editor: Carla Hall

Editor: Jane Palmer

Proofreader: Heather Wilcox

Indexer: Jane Palmer

DEDICATION

I dedicate this book to my wonderful son-in-law, Jason McKay—a Marine, a certified public accountant, and now a registered nurse. I couldn't be more proud of you or more pleased to have you as part of a profession I love.

ACKNOWLEDGMENTS

I would like to acknowledge and thank all those mentors, role models, colleagues, family members, and friends who have shaped my personal leadership journey. Your support, guidance, and love have made such a difference in my life and my career.

ABOUT THE AUTHOR

Carol J. Huston, DPA, MSN, RN, FAAN
Carol Jorgensen Huston has been a Professor in the School of Nursing at California State University, Chico (CSUC), since 1982 and assumed the position of Director of the School of Nursing from 2010–15. She currently teaches classes on leadership, management, health finance, and health systems part time as Emerita Professor. Huston was named one of seven CSUC Master Teachers in 1999, 2000, and 2001, the CSUC Outstanding Teacher for the 2001–02 academic year, and the CSUC Outstanding Professor for the 2008–09 academic year.

Huston is co-author of six textbooks on leadership, management, and professional issues in nursing (a total of 19 editions) and has published more than 100 articles and editorials in leading professional journals. Her co-authored book *Leadership Roles and Management Functions in Nursing*, now in its ninth edition, has been translated into four languages, and *Management Decision Making for Nurses* received an *AJN* Book of the Year award. The fourth edition of *Professional Issues in Nursing: Challenges and Opportunities* published in 2017.

In addition, Huston has given more than 300 presentations at nursing and healthcare conferences worldwide. She is also a successful grant writer and has been primary investigator or co-investigator of multiple grants. Huston has served on the Enloe Medical Center (Chico, California) Board of Trustees since 2012 and as Chair of the board since 2016.

Huston is a Fellow in the American Academy of Nursing. In addition, she served as the 2007–09 President of the Honor Society of Nursing, Sigma Theta Tau International (STTI). As President, she was responsible for strategic planning, program implementation, and fiduciary oversight of approximately 130,000 nurses in more than 470 chapters in more than 90 countries. In addition, she served as Co-chairperson of the 2010 International Year of the Nurse (IYNurse) Initiative, a global partnership effort of STTI, Nightingale Initiative for Global Health, and Nightingale Museum of London. She has served as lead faculty for STTI's Experienced Nurse Faculty Leadership Academy since 2014 and is Facilitator and Coordinator for STTI's Institute for Global Healthcare Leadership, which launched in Washington, DC, in September 2016.

TABLE OF CONTENTS

LEADERSHIP LESSONS

ALL NURSES CAN BE NURSE LEADERS

I didn't always perceive myself as a leader. I knew I wanted to make a difference in the world and in the profession I loved but was far less clear about the path I might take to make that happen. Indeed, my passion, genuine caring for others, propensity for risk-taking, and willingness to work hard far exceeded any formal leadership training or skills I had. As a result, my personal leadership journey was filled with unexpected twists and turns; missed chances, as well as incredible opportunities; and disappointments as well as successes. In other words, it was hard. It was also amazing and life-altering. The knowledge I gained from incredible mentors and role models, as well as experience, provided me with the tools I needed to succeed in multiple leadership roles. The lessons I learned along the journey resulted in extensive personal growth and self-discovery that have changed my life forever.

My guess is that many nurses want to become leaders but feel overwhelmed and are not sure where to begin. I wrote this book for them. It examines the need for leadership development in nursing, discusses what leadership means—including how it means different things in different situations and with different people—and emphasizes the importance of good followers to the leadership equation.

The book is organized with nine sections detailing valuable leadership lessons I learned along my own leadership journey. I learned many of these lessons the hard way and have purposely shared stories where I encountered frustration and failure as a leader. My hope in sharing these stories and suggestions is that readers will gain confidence in their own ability to lead, reflect on their own leadership strengths and weaknesses, and establish new goals and a plan for their future leadership development.

The nine leadership lessons I've learned along my own leadership journey are:

1. Find a Mentor and Positive Role Models to Share Your Journey

2. Be Self-Aware and Authentic

3. Be Able to Laugh at Yourself and Leave Your Ego at Home in a Jar

4. Be Visionary, Take Risks, and Ask for Permission Only When Necessary

5. Maintain Personal Power: Keep Gas in the Tank and Money in the Bank

6. Choose Your Battles Carefully

7. Perfect the "Art" of Communication

8. Appreciate and Empower Followers

9. Set Priorities and Enjoy the Journey

I would also argue that developing leadership skills is no longer optional for nurses. Healthcare is big business, and nurse leaders are now expected to have expertise in budgeting, finance, and marketing. They're also expected to be skilled communicators and team builders and to be visionary and proactive in preparing for new threats we didn't think much about several decades ago, such as terrorism, biological warfare, and emerging global pandemics.

At the organizational level, nurse leaders are expected to address high staff turnover, staffing shortages, limited resources, quality mandates, and inter-personal conflicts that all too often result in unhealthy workplace cultures and incivility. Nurse leaders are also challenged to balance the "human element" with rapidly emerging healthcare technologies and to ensure that both the art and science of nursing are maintained in our patient care. The contemporary leadership expectations of nurses, then, are extremely high.

Unfortunately, as I have traveled the world, many nurses have told me they believe their leadership skills are inadequately developed for the roles they already hold. In some cases, it's because they had inadequate formal education or training in leadership and management. Others had such train-ing but didn't really pay attention, believing they would never hold a formal leadership role. Still others have shared that they were taught basic leader-ship principles but weren't prepared for how quickly they would be expected to assume leadership positions as new nurses.

Fortunately, most nurses have better leadership skills than they give themselves credit for. Many of these nurses have had to learn these skills the hard way—by trial and error. When we're talking about human lives, the consequences of doing so can be costly.

I personally believe that all nurses can and must be leaders. I also believe that leadership is a choice. Although early leadership theorists suggested that the propensity for leadership was inborn, most contemporary theorists argue that one can choose to be a leader or a follower.

Some people *do* have certain characteristics or personality traits that may make it easier for them to lead. For example, some people, even at very young ages, are more fearless. Others are naturally more outgoing; they're more curious and take more risks. But not all leaders need to be gregarious by nature; there is a lot of room for quiet leadership. In fact, some of the most effective leaders I know are individuals who didn't seek out that role—they simply grew into it because they stepped forth to do what had to be done when no one else would.

Being a nurse leader, however, is difficult when resources are limited, performance expectations are high, and obligations to patients, employers, and self are in conflict. It also takes time to develop the skills and self-confidence that are an important part of the leadership role. Author Malcolm Gladwell

"The truth is, there are a lot of bad leaders (bosses, managers, whatever you want to call them) and people suffer greatly at their hands. Organizations, clients, and communities probably suffer as well. Often this occurs, however, because many people simply don't know **HOW** to be a better leader."

—Rob Jenkins (2017, para. 4)

(as cited in Bradberry, 2017) suggests that mastery of anything requires 10,000 hours of tireless focus. Thus, development of leadership skills typically requires time, energy, and willingness to assume the role.

Unfortunately, many people are promoted into leadership positions without having demonstrated even a slight ability to lead (Keating, 2016). Instead, these promotions occurred because an individual demonstrated some ability to manage people or tasks. Jenkins (2017) agrees, noting that the way it works in most organizations is that people who are good at their jobs receive a promotion and suddenly find themselves in a leadership position without having any experience in that role.

Leadership and management, however, are not the same thing. Leaders are individuals who are out front—moving forward, taking risks, and challenging the status quo. They have vision as well as the energy to create a better future. In contrast, managers have a certain amount of status, power, and authority due to the formal position they hold. In other words, subordinates *must* follow managers, because it's an expectation of their job.

Kerr (2015, para. 2) also differentiates between leadership and management: "Leaders look forward and imagine the possibilities that the future may bring in order to set direction. Managers monitor and adjust today's work, regularly looking backward to ensure that current goals and objectives are being met."

"MANAGEMENT IS EFFICIENCY IN CLIMBING THE LADDER OF SUCCESS;

LEADERSHIP DETERMINES WHETHER THE LADDER IS LEANING AGAINST THE RIGHT WALL."

—Stephen R. Covey (1989, p. 101)

Leadership, then, does not come from position or title; leaders accomplish things because others follow them willingly. Indeed, Keating (2016) suggests that the only thing that makes you a leader is leading. Rockwell (2016) concurs, noting that authority, position, and title won't make you a leader. Instead of worrying about being a leader, Rockwell suggests that an individual should worry about being a person worthy of being followed—because all it takes to stop being a leader is to have your followers choose to stop following you.

The reality is that all nurses need well-developed leadership skills to address the complexities of 21st-century healthcare. The Institute of Medicine (IOM, 2010, p. 221) agrees: "Although the public is not used to viewing nurses as leaders, and not all nurses begin their careers with thoughts of becoming a leader, all nurses must be leaders in the design, implementation, and evaluation of—as well as advocacy for—the ongoing reforms to the system that will be needed." The IOM (p. 225) goes on to say:

> *Nurses must understand that their leadership is as important to providing quality care as is their technical ability to deliver care at the bedside in a safe and effective manner. They must lead in improving work processes on the front lines; creating new integrated practice models; working with others, from organizational policy makers to state legislators, to craft practice*

policy and legislation that allows nurses to work to their fullest capacity; leading curriculum changes to prepare the nursing workforce to meet community and patient needs; translating and applying research findings into practice and developing functional models of care; and serving on institutional and policy-making boards where critical decisions affecting patients are made.

Melnyk, Malloch, and Gallagher-Ford (2017, p. 30) outline qualities of effective nurse leaders:

Nurse leaders also need to understand and clearly articulate the inextricable connectedness of nurse engagement, productivity, and retention with caring and quality outcomes, which ultimately drive satisfaction and the financial well-being of the organization. Therefore, nurse leaders must be creative, innovative, entrepreneurial, and resourceful in garnering new resources and strategizing to maintain the core nursing value of caring to increase efficiency and to drive quality outcomes.

"**Nursing leadership is vitally important to our profession, now more than ever. I do not mean traditional leadership with its hierarchy of formal positions, but rather, all nurses everywhere engaged in grassroots leadership.**"

—Linda Gobis (2016, para. 1)

Nurses can no longer argue that only nurses in formal management positions need leadership skills. All nurses can be nurse leaders, and part of their professional responsibility is to gain the skills needed to successfully assume that role.

REFERENCES

Bradberry, T. (2017, January 28). 10 harsh lessons that will make you more successful [Blog post]. Retrieved from http://www.huffingtonpost.com/dr-travis-bradberry/10-harsh-lessons-that-wil_b_14422346.html

Covey, S. R. (1989). *The seven habits of highly effective people*. New York, NY: Simon and Schuster.

Gobis, L. (2016, December 30). Nurses as leaders: At all levels, in all settings. *Wisconsin Nurses Association*. Retrieved from http://wisconsinnurses.org/nurses-leaders-levels-settings/

Institute of Medicine. (2010, October). *The future of nursing: Leading change, advancing health*. Washington DC: National Academies Press.

Jenkins, R. (2017, March 28). Four huge obstacles to good leadership [Blog post]. Retrieved from http://9virtues.com/blog.cfm?month=3&year=2017

Keating, S. (2016, November 21). Managing stuff, leading people [Blog post]. Retrieved from https://stevekeating.me/2016/11/21/managing-stuff-leading-people

Kerr, J. (2015, August 3). The leadership checklist: 10 principles that make leading easier. *Inc.* Retrieved from https://www.inc.com/james-kerr/the-leadership-checklist-10-principles-that-make-leading-easier.html

Melnyk, B., Malloch, K., & Gallagher-Ford, L. (2017). Developing effective leaders to meet 21st century health care challenges. In C. Huston (Ed.), *Professional issues in nursing: Challenges and opportunities* (Chapter 3). Philadelphia, PA: Wolters Kluwer.

Rockwell, D. (2016, October 30). 10 ways to be a leader people choose to follow [Blog post]. Retrieved from https://leadershipfreak.blog/2016/10/30/10-ways-to-be-a-leader-people-choose-to-follow/

1

FIND A MENTOR AND POSITIVE ROLE MODELS TO SHARE YOUR JOURNEY

Leadership Lesson #1 is the importance of finding a mentor and positive role models to guide you on your leadership journey. *Mentoring* is an intense, positive, one-on-one relationship between an experienced professional and a less experienced novice. Mentors support, guide, and protect novices and help them learn and do whatever is necessary to be successful in their new role.

Many novice nurses need time to learn the complexities of the professional nursing role, and having the protection of a mentor is critical to their success. Unfortunately, nursing has earned a reputation for not supporting its young, and the literature suggests that reputation is likely well-deserved. Having a mentor show you the ropes, tell you about hidden organizational taboos, and give you that "in" we all needed as new nurses is so important to career success.

But it is not just new nurses who need mentors. Mentors are also helpful for experienced nurses who are in new roles or settings where they may not fully understand the formal and informal power structure of the organization or the expectations of their new role.

The best example I can give you comes from my first faculty meeting as a new academic. I had come to academe from a middle-management hospital position, where I was generally recognized as a successful department head and where my opinions and thoughts were typically sought out and valued.

The topic for discussion at my first faculty meeting was pass-fail grading in clinical courses. I couldn't wait to jump in and offer my uninformed opinion—which I did almost immediately after the discussion started. As you might guess, this was a mistake. I can still remember the silence in the room. This group of bright, experienced nurse educators all turned and looked at me. Then one of the most senior faculty members turned to me and said, "Perhaps after you've been here for a while and really understand the issues under discussion, your opinion will matter more."

I was shocked by what was clearly a personal affront. Yet, while incivility is never acceptable, she was right, at least on some level. I was a newcomer to the organization, and I had not yet paid my dues in terms of understanding the big issues of academe, which are very different from those in the clinical arena. Having a mentor might have helped me understand the politics of this new organization—who held informal and formal power and what alliances needed to be built. I also think a mentor would have reminded me of the importance of "paying dues" first to gain credibility.

Having a mentor is only valuable, however, if the relationship is honest and constructive. And that means telling you the truth, even if it hurts sometimes. Self-image and self-perception may not be accurate. A mentor must be able to tell you how others perceive you, even when it's different from how you perceive yourself. I was very fortunate to find my first mentor after I joined academe in 1982. It wasn't always easy to hear what she had to say, but it always made me a better person and a stronger leader.

You'll also want to find a mentor who is willing to be your cheerleader. In other words, you want someone who will inspire you to stretch and become more than you thought possible. I'm not talking about someone who sets impossible goals for you, but having someone really believe in you and push you to think bigger is a tremendous gift. My mentor always had a vision for me that was far greater than I had for myself.

For example, I can remember the first time she suggested we write a book together. I was a junior faculty member, and I remember looking at her and laughing because it seemed like such a monumental task. Writing a 75-page master's thesis was very difficult, although I loved to write and was good at it. With her vision and my willingness to work hard, we made a great team and wrote 11 books together. I've since written eight by myself.

Early on, my mentor also suggested different things I could do "once I had earned my doctoral degree." Again, I would just look at her and think how unfeasible a return to school was when I had a young family and a full-time job. But once my mentor planted that seed, I did *start* to think about it. And once you begin to do that, things start to happen. I did go back to school, and once I had achieved my goal of earning a doctoral degree, many of the things my mentor envisioned for me became possible.

And finally, at least 15 years ago, my mentor said very casually, "I think you should run for President of Sigma Theta Tau International (STTI) someday." Again, I laughed and shook my head. STTI was certainly my professional association of choice, and I had dedicated years in service at the local and regional levels. But my fear of public speaking and lack of self-confidence that I could do the role well made that goal seem unreachable. Yet, 5 years later (2007-09), I did serve as STTI President, and it was one of the most amazing experiences of my life.

I often wonder whether I would have achieved what I have in my life without my mentor. I'm not saying that it didn't take hard work and energy on my part, but I'm not sure I would have seen the possibilities without her. I think her vision and willingness to be my cheerleader made the difference.

Indeed, Myers (2016) notes that mentorship requires strong commitment and a lot of effort from both parties. "Too many young professionals fail to

realize that mentorship is a two-way street. You have to deliver tremendous value to your mentor as well, and that often means working longer and harder than those around you" (para. 7).

Clearly, having one or more mentors is a vital part of a young person's leadership journey. Yet Myers (2016) suggests that many young people lack enthusiasm toward the concept of mentorship. Indeed, some even chafe at the idea that they need someone to help open doors for them for career success. He says that the end results are more than worth it and encourages young people to ask and take advantage of what mentors can offer.

So, how do you choose a mentor? Ashley (2015) suggests it's not just about choosing someone with relevant experience. Instead, she says you should select someone who can offer you what you need right now—which may very well be different from what you needed 12 months ago or what you will need in the next 12 months. In addition, because needs can and do constantly change, the goals of the mentoring relationship will likely need to be reviewed and refined regularly, or you may need to find additional mentors with different skill sets.

"I firmly believe that mentorship is the best path to career success, hands down. The benefits that you can gain from a good mentor relationship can outweigh grad school, natural ability, and even dumb luck. The key is to have the foresight and humility to ask to be mentored. If you start there, you'll find that there are plenty of accelerators in your life who can add value. More importantly, you can take it upon yourself to add tremendous value for them. In doing so, you'll ensure that you get the most out of the mentor relationship and find success in your life and career."

—Chris Myers (2016, para. 10)

"The misconception, however, is that a mentor relationship has to be a formal agreement with predetermined outcomes that are measurable. It is true, a formal mentor relationship will define outcomes. However, the nature of a mentor relationship means that there is a degree of flexibility required. Initially determined outcomes most likely will change during the course of the relationship."

—Rebecca Fraser (2017, para. 2)

Ashley (2015, para. 2) suggests answering the following questions to help you determine who might be the best mentor for you:

» Are you looking for help in relation to specific aspects of your career, or your current or future role?

» Are you trying to take your career or leadership to the next level?

» Are you looking to develop your own strengths, skills, and experience for the next 5 years?

» Or is it more about getting support for some specific challenges you are facing now—personally, or in your role or career?

Being open to having a mentor who challenges you to look at things differently is also important. Unfortunately, most of us seek out collaborations with individuals who think and look like us. While it's important for collaborators to be compatible, associating only with clones limits your ability to understand new viewpoints and experience the richness you find in diversity.

Leadership Lesson #1 also suggests that positive role models are important. That's because positive role models are contagious. The inverse is true as well: If you primarily associate with disgruntled, tired, and frustrated nurses, then that is the behavior you are more likely to adopt. Fortunately, there are many wonderful, positive nursing role models. You just need to find them.

The best example I can give you of the impact of positive role models was at one of the first STTI conventions I attended as a fairly new nurse. I arrived late to the luncheon and therefore took one of the few remaining seats at a table at the front of the room. Everyone welcomed me warmly and began introducing themselves. You can imagine my shock when I realized that I had sat down with some of the most eminent nursing leaders in this country at that time. I simply felt overwhelmed and inadequate. These were people I had studied in school, and I thought of them as theoretical icons, not real people.

The amazing part about this experience was that all of them not only welcomed me to the table but actively involved me in conversation. They made me feel like an important part of the convention as well as nursing. I have often thought about this luncheon. I recognized that being a national nursing leader doesn't mean being some distant theoretical icon—it's about being real and accessible to others. What a valuable lesson for me to learn so early in my career.

REFERENCES

Ashley, S. (2015, August 10). How to choose the right mentor for you. *Human Resources Director*. Retrieved from http://www.hcamag.com/opinion/how-to-choose-the-right-mentor-for-you-203863.aspx

Fraser, R. (2017). A guide to mentoring for career success. *Undercover Recruiter*. Retrieved from http://theundercoverrecruiter.com/mentoring-career-success/

Myers, C. (2016, February 21). Mentorship is key to career success for young professionals. *Forbes*. Retrieved from https://www.forbes.com/sites/chrismyers/2016/02/21/mentorship-is-key-to-career-success-for-young-professionals/#61fda37b21b8

2

BE
SELF-
AWARE
AND
AUTHENTIC

Leadership Lesson #2 is the importance of being self-aware and authentic. Indeed, Bird (2017) posits that lack of self-awareness is a classic leadership Achilles' heel and that the long road of failure is littered with leaders who lacked self-awareness.

Eblin (2017, para. 3) agrees, suggesting that great leaders are always self-aware and intentional. "They tune into what's going on around them and notice the physical, mental, and emotional reactions they're having to what's going on around them. Based on that awareness, they are then intentional about what they're going to do or not do next."

Being truly self-aware, though, is much harder to do in real life than it sounds. That's because self-awareness requires a person to dredge up and reexamine painful, life-altering experiences and to consider how they have influenced who the individual has become.

Being self-aware is a hallmark of a leader. In fact, one of the newer leadership theories is the idea of *authentic leadership*. Authentic leadership suggests that in order to lead, leaders must be true to themselves and their values and act accordingly. In authentic leadership, then, the leader's principles and conviction to act accordingly are what inspire followers.

"BE YOURSELF. EVERYONE ELSE IS ALREADY TAKEN."

—Oscar Wilde (as cited in Goodreads, para. 1)

McGoff (2017, para. 4) agrees, suggesting that living in integrity and "being your word" are essential for others to trust you. This trust promotes interconnectedness, intimacy, and synchronicity and leads to a feeling of oneness and unity. Indeed, trust is considered by many to be the foundation or the basic building block for healthy relationships and effective, functional teams (Melnyk, Malloch, & Gallagher-Ford, 2017). Wise leaders know that trust is critical to their success, and they work every day to attain and sustain it.

Authentic leadership, though, can be very hard to deliver. It takes a lot of courage to be true to one's convictions when external forces or peer pressure encourages us to do something we believe is morally inappropriate. Often, when we turn on the news, we see examples of nonauthentic leaders—the world-class athlete who advocates healthy lifestyles and is found to be using steroids or the political or religious figure who preaches morality and becomes involved in a sex or financial scandal. We also see leaders at the organizational level who say they care about their staff—or faculty who claim to be student-centered—but their actions suggest otherwise. Whether these leaders lack self-awareness or simply choose not to act in accordance with what they say they value, the bottom line is that leaders who are not authentic will eventually lose their followers.

"Self-awareness isn't one of those big marquee leadership qualities like vision, charisma, strategic thinking or the ability to speak eloquently to an audience the size of a small city ... but it's a quieter ancillary quality that enables the high-octane ones to work. To use a chemistry concept, it's a psychological catalyst."

—Victor Lipman (2013, para. 6)

McGoff (2017, para. 1) agrees, suggesting that integrity is about honoring your word as your life. "When a person of integrity gives their word, or makes a commitment, they follow through, with no exceptions. When integrity is present, it is one of the most powerful characteristics in any person or organization; however, when absent, it can be one of the most damaging."

People know when they are not being authentic. Researchers from Harvard, Columbia, and Northwestern found that when people failed to behave authentically, they experienced a heightened state of discomfort that's usually associated with immorality. In fact, people who weren't true to themselves were so distraught that they often felt a strong desire to cleanse themselves physically (Bradberry, 2016). Simply put, "Our brains know when we're living a lie, and like all lies, being inauthentic causes nothing but harm" (para. 4).

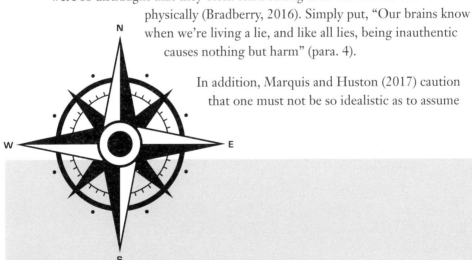

In addition, Marquis and Huston (2017) caution that one must not be so idealistic as to assume that all leaders strive to be authentic. Indeed, many are flawed at times. Leaders may be deceitful and trustworthy, greedy and generous, cowardly and brave. To assume that all good leaders are good people is foolhardy and makes us blind to the human condition. Future leadership theory may well focus on why leaders behave badly and why some followers continue to follow bad leaders.

In addition, part of self-awareness is understanding what values you hold dear. Thum (2013) suggests that personal values are the general expression of what is most important for you: They are like categories for all your preferences in life. It is important to be self-aware regarding your values so that you can begin to recognize how they influence your decision-making.

When we lack clarity about our values, feelings take over, and we tend to make emotional choices. Gausepohl (2017) suggests that followers need to see the facts and logic backing up the choices of their leaders to trust them. When logic or reason does not exist, followers can become confused or uncertain regarding future plans or the validity of the decisions over time, slowly chiseling away at the leader's effectiveness.

Marquis and Huston (2017) note, however, that no matter how self-aware we are, value judgments will always play a part in a person's decision-making, either consciously or subconsciously. The alternatives generated and the final choices are limited by each person's value system. For some,

"When words and actions match, when one is perceived as authentic, and when humility and reflection are common actions ... trust will flourish. The benefits and rewards of relationships forged from trust are immeasurable, and it is in every nurse leader's best interest to cultivate this attribute."

–Bernadette Melnyk, Kathy Malloch, and Lynn Gallagher-Ford (2017, p. 35)

certain choices are not possible because of personal beliefs. Because values also influence perceptions, they invariably influence information gathering, information processing, and the final outcome. Values also determine which problems in one's personal or professional life will be addressed or ignored.

Sometimes, too, if people are not self-aware, they fail to determine what the desired end goal is. And then, even though they may achieve incredible things, they don't celebrate them, because they never knew what they were looking for in the first place. For example, some nurses seek a level of perfection in their clinical practice or leadership skills that is unrealistic. Thus, they just keep working harder and longer—losing balance in their personal and professional lives and never feeling satisfied.

To become a leader, then, individuals must spend critical time in self-reflection to better understand what their most important beliefs and values are and then act in accordance with these values. Once individuals have this clarity, they can live life more confidently because there is nothing to hide. They know that being genuine is the cornerstone of trust they have with their followers.

"BECOMING A LEADER ... IS SYNONYMOUS WITH BECOMING YOURSELF. IT'S PRECISELY THAT SIMPLE, AND IT'S ALSO THAT DIFFICULT."

—Warren Bennis (as cited in Ignatius, 2015, para. 1)

REFERENCES

Bird, S. (2017, January 12). Trump needs to learn from Lincoln [Blog post]. Retrieved from http://www.huffingtonpost.com/shelley-bird/trump-needs-to-learn-from_b_14113806.html

Bradberry, T. (2016, December 31). 10 unmistakable habits of utterly authentic people [Blog post]. Retrieved from http://www.huffingtonpost.com/dr-travis-bradberry/10-unmistakable-habits-of_b_13772102.html

Eblin, S. (2017, January 19). The ten behaviors of strong personal leadership [Blog post]. Retrieved from https://eblingroup.com/blog/the-ten-behaviors-of-strong-personal-leadership/

Gausepohl, S. (2017, February 15). 5 common leadership mistakes you're probably making. *Business News Daily*. Retrieved from http://www.businessnewsdaily.com/8517-common-leadership-mistakes.html

Goodreads Inc. (2017). Oscar Wilde quotes. Retrieved from http://www.goodreads.com/quotes/19884-be-yourself-everyone-else-is-already-taken

Ignatius, A. (2015, May). Becoming a leader, becoming yourself. *Harvard Business Review*. Retrieved from https://hbr.org/2015/05/becoming-a-leader-becoming-yourself

Lipman, V. (2013, November 18). All successful leaders need this quality: Self-awareness. *Forbes*. Retrieved from https://www.forbes.com/sites/victorlipman/2013/11/18/all-successful-leaders-need-this-quality-self-awareness/#61e51581f068

Marquis, B., & Huston, C. (2017). *Leadership roles and management functions in nursing* (9th ed.). Philadelphia, PA: Wolters Kluwer.

McGoff, C. (2017, February 23). Why integrity is the foundation of a peak performance leader. *SmartBrief*. Retrieved from http://www.smartbrief.com/original/2017/02/why-integrity-foundation-peak-performance-leader

Melnyk, B., Malloch, K., & Gallagher-Ford, L. (2017). Developing effective leaders to meet 21st century health care challenges. In C. Huston (Ed.), *Professional issues in nursing: Challenges and opportunities* (Chapter 3). Philadelphia, PA: Wolters Kluwer.

Thum, M. (2013, February 22). Do you know your personal values? [Blog post]. Retrieved from http://www.myrkothum.com/personal-values/

3

BE ABLE TO
LAUGH AT
YOURSELF
AND LEAVE
YOUR EGO
AT HOME
IN A JAR

Leadership Lesson #3 is to lighten up a little and not take life quite so seriously. In other words, be able to laugh at yourself, and leave your ego at home in a jar. This doesn't mean that we shouldn't recognize and celebrate achievements by ourselves or others. We all need to be recognized for our talents and accomplishments.

But humility is an underrecognized leadership trait, especially when it is a true part of character. Haden and Jenkins (2017, para. 11) agree: "Leaders who embrace and seek to internalize the virtue of humility do not simply fade into the background, as some might imagine. Ultimately, they are the fittest, the strongest, and the most capable of leading."

The reality, though, is that sometimes we take ourselves far too seriously. Indeed, most people take themselves far more seriously than anyone else does. Ringer (n.d.) suggests it's very easy to fall into the trap of blowing things out of proportion, demanding perfection, and acting as though your needs are at the center of the universe. When this happens, you lose yourself, your center, and your perspective.

Taking ourselves too seriously also reduces our risk-taking, because we are so afraid of failure that we make no attempt to succeed. This fear of making a mistake or not being perfect can be paralyzing. We are all human and make mistakes, and being embarrassed by the mistakes we make is a universal experience. "It takes confidence to look failure in the face and keep moving forward because, if we are confident in ourselves and our ability, we look at failure as part of the fine-tuning process" (Quy, 2017, para. 13).

"YOU MISS 100% OF THE SHOTS YOU DON'T TAKE."

—Wayne Gretzky
(as cited in
BrainyQuote, n.d.)

In taking our mistakes so seriously, we forget that most mistakes are recoverable. That doesn't mean they don't hurt or aren't embarrassing. For example, several years ago, I did a presentation on nursing's public image as part of a regional research conference. In my conclusion, I included a slide of a very small Chihuahua standing face to face with a very large Great Dane. The large-font caption on the slide was, "Never be afraid to say what you think." Little did I know that, inserted on the slide in a very small font, were several *very* profane words coming out of the Chihuahua's mouth. The font was too small to read on my small computer screen at home, but it was very readable on the large screen at the front of the auditorium. I had no idea what was on my slide until I heard my audience collectively gasp and begin whispering about what they saw on the screen.

I have probably never been more embarrassed in my professional life. I did gain a lot of insight about checking and double-checking slides for every presentation I have given since. But I think the most valuable leadership lesson I learned from this experience was that it's OK to be fallible—followers will forgive you, and the key is simply to acknowledge your fallibilities and move on. It would have done no good to continue to beat myself up over something I couldn't undo. Instead, I apologized profusely to my followers and, since then, have shared the mistake I made with many others who wished they could undo a poor choice or a lapse in judgment in their lives.

"**UNLESS YOU'RE A HERO IN AN EPIC TALE, YOUR ACTIONS RARELY DETERMINE THE FATE OF THE WORLD.**"

—Chrysta Bairre (2011, para. 12)

Another part of giving up some ego is realizing that we likely never have as much control over things as we would like to think we do. In fact, I often remind myself that control is only an illusion and that life can change in the blink of an eye. Wise leaders recognize that while we cannot control all the bad things that happen in our lives, we can control how we respond to the outcomes. Whining about how unfair a situation is does little to help. Instead, being able to pick up the pieces, making the best out of a tough situation, and moving forward demonstrate true courage, an important leadership characteristic.

In addition, many of us focus on the problems in our lives and assume that everyone else has things easier. The reality, though, is that life is full of challenges for everyone, and if we all placed our problems in a pile, we would likely want our own problems back.

Eblin (2017) concurs, suggesting that great leaders are grateful and constantly recognize and acknowledge the good things in their life. "They understand that even on days when it feels like everything is going wrong, there is always something that's going right" (para. 13).

Similarly, Kux (n.d., para. 7) says that if you need a reminder that your problems aren't as big as they seem and you want to readjust your perspective, get out of the city and look at the stars:

The universe is larger than you can imagine. It is filled with burning balls of gas, galaxies and solar systems beyond counting, and (in all likelihood) thousands of other civilizations fighting their own wars and facing their own challenges. In a very real sense, you are insignificant. What better reason could there be not to take your life to [sic] seriously? The only thing that really matters is enjoying your life as much as you can and helping other people do the same.

"The more we know, the less we realize we really know. The deeper down the rabbit hole we go, the further there is to go. Until we decide that's quite far enough, thank you very much."

—Catherine Simmons (2017, para. 5)

We also all need to laugh more. Dwight D. Eisenhower said, "A sense of humor is part of the art of leadership, of getting along with people, and of getting things done" (Eisenhower, as cited in Smith, 2013, para. 1). In addition, Michael Kerr, an international business speaker, cites several surveys suggesting that humor can be at least one of the keys to success (Kerr, as cited in Smith, 2013). One survey found that 91% of executives believe a sense of humor is important for career advancement, while 84% believe that people with a good sense of humor do a better job (Robert Half International, as cited in Smith, 2013). Another study found that the two most desirable traits in leaders were a strong work ethic and a good sense of humor (Bell Leadership Institute, as cited in Smith, 2013).

Finally, it's OK to let your pretenses down occasionally and be human. I think women are at greater risk of this need to be the perfect nurse, the perfect spouse, the perfect parent, and the perfect employee. The reality is that anytime we seek perfection in one role, it is at the expense of another role, and that search for perfection is exhausting. When I think back on the experiences in my life that I let pass me by because I was afraid I might not be capable or that I might be embarrassed, it makes me sad. I also look back at opportunities I had to do things that would have been fun—but I didn't do them because I didn't want to put on that swimming suit, my hair wasn't done, or I thought someone might think I was being silly. What a shame to have missed out on those opportunities.

REFERENCES

Bairre, C. (2011, December 30). Don't take life too seriously. *Live, Love, Work.* Retrieved from http://www.liveandlovework.com/2011/12/30/dont-take-life-too-seriously/

BrainyQuote. (n.d.). Wayne Gretzky quotes. Retrieved from https://www.brainyquote.com/quotes/quotes/w/waynegretz378694.html

Eblin, S. (2017, January 19). The ten behaviors of strong personal leadership [Blog post]. Retrieved from https://eblingroup.com/blog/the-ten-behaviors-of-strong-personal-leadership/

Haden, N. K., & Jenkins, R. (2017, January 16). Dr. King and the power of humility [Blog post]. Retrieved from http://www.9virtues.com/blogpost.cfm?id=10064

Kux, S. (n.d.). 6 reasons not to take life so seriously. *Lifehack.* Retrieved from http://www.lifehack.org/articles/productivity/6-reasons-not-take-life-seriously.html

Quy, L. (2017, March 15). 10 hard skills to learn that will last a lifetime. *SmartBrief.* Retrieved from http://www.smartbrief.com/original/2017/03/10-hard-skills-learn-will-last-lifetime?utm_source=brief

Ringer, J. (n.d.). Taking myself too seriously: Suggestions for reclaiming perspective [Blog post]. Retrieved from http://www.judyringer.com/resources/articles/taking-myself-too-seriously-suggestions-for-reclaiming-perspective.php

Simmons, C. (2017, January 13). A little philosophy to help us take life less seriously. Elephant Journal. Retrieved from https://www.elephantjournal.com/2017/01/a-little-philosophy-to-help-us-take-life-less-seriously/

Smith, J. (2013, May 3). 10 reasons why humor is a key to success at work. *Forbes.* Retrieved from https://www.forbes.com/sites/jacquelynsmith/2013/05/03/10-reasons-why-humor-is-a-key-to-success-at-work/#5d0444705c90

4

BE
VISIONARY,
TAKE RISKS,
AND ASK FOR
PERMISSION
ONLY WHEN
NECESSARY

Leadership Lesson #4 is to be visionary, take risks, and ask for permission only when absolutely necessary. Individuals without vision rarely become leaders. When leaders espouse a powerful vision that other people want to share, followers are motivated to take action. Carton (2017, para. 11) agrees, noting that leaders must

> Paint a grand picture of what it is that we're all trying to achieve, this destination that we're all trying to reach. But just as important—and also more time consuming and requiring even more investment—is that they communicate about how each employee in the organization can get a sense of how their work connects to the organization's mission or vision.

One might question whether leaders are simply better able to see the future than others or whether they actually create the future they have envisioned. In either case, vision has little value if there is no action component. Hyatt (2012, para. 1) agrees that vision and strategy are both important to career success, but he argues that there is a priority to them: "Vision always comes first. Always. If you have a clear vision, you will eventually attract the right strategy. If you don't have a clear vision, no strategy will save you."

"There's nothing more demoralizing than a leader who can't clearly articulate why we're doing what we're doing."

—James Kouzes and Barry Posner (as cited in Heathfield, 2016)

Similarly, Melnyk, Malloch, and Gallagher-Ford (2017, p. 34) note:

> *There is nothing more important to achieving success*
> *than a potent dream/vision and an ability to inspire*
> *that vision in the team. The change efforts of many*
> *leaders fail because they focus too much on process and*
> *not enough on an exciting vision, although it does need*
> *to be recognized that vision without execution will also*
> *deter success. A motivational vision/dream will keep the*
> *energy of the leader and the team going when barriers,*
> *challenges, or fears are slowing or preventing outcomes*
> *from being achieved.*

The risk-taking, however, needed to become a leader may be even more difficult than the visioning. Quy (2017, para. 13) says:

> *Many people fear failure so much that we shuffle along*
> *in life until we accidentally stumble onto something at*
> *which we are good. Success can be misleading because*
> *it often is not what really fuels us. Such success is based*
> *in complacency because we are too scared of failure to*
> *pursue the type of work that would provide value and*
> *meaning.*

"That's what vision does for leadership; it gives the team direction, and helps them to focus on understanding what it really takes to get the job done. It inspires. It creates. Like the player on a team who makes others around him better, vision helps make everyone see the same picture—clearly."

—Kary Zate
(2011, para. 7)

In fact, we all have a different risk-taking quotient. Some people really are risk-adverse, and some love the thrill of being on the edge and taking risks. The reality is that taking risks is a big part of leadership. But there are risks, and then there are risks. The risk itself shouldn't be the thrill: What makes the risk worthwhile should be the possibility of positive outcomes associated with taking that risk. Likewise, risk-taking that is more likely than not to result in personal or professional harm is rarely wise. But not taking any risks is worse than taking too many. Conformity is the opposite of leadership, because no one is willing to take the risk of leading.

That's probably why *thought leadership* has emerged as one of the newest leadership theories in the 21st century. In many ways, thought leadership is the opposite of group think. A *thought leader* is a person who is recognized among his or her peers for innovative ideas and who demonstrates the confidence to promote those ideas. Thus, thought leadership refers to any situation in which one individual convinces another to consider a new idea, product, or way of looking at things. Thought leaders then challenge the status quo and attract followers not by any promise of representation or empowerment but by their risk-taking and vision in terms of being innovative (Marquis & Huston, 2017). In addition, the ideas put forth by thought leaders typically are future-oriented and make a significant impact. They are also generally problem-oriented, which increases their value to both individuals and organizations.

"CREATIVITY IS THE NEW CURRENCY, SO, ARE YOU CREDITED WITH NEW THOUGHTS OR OVERDRAWN IN OLD THINKING?"

—Onyi Anyado (2015, para. 13)

Thought leadership requires risk-taking, because people like stability in their lives and generally resist changes to the status quo. Thought leaders suggest, though, that just because we've done something one way for a long time doesn't mean it's the best way. Thus, thought leaders often meet some resistance, at least initially, to their ideas. It's not personal. Resistance is just the normal and expected response to change that almost always occurs.

According to Bradberry (2017), the first step in leading change is always the hardest. Once you take that step, anxiety and fear often dissipate in the name of action. "People that dive headfirst into taking that brutal first step aren't

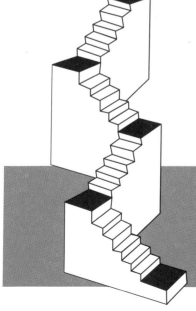

any stronger than the rest of us; they've simply learned that it yields great results.… Procrastination only prolongs their suffering" (para. 7).

Leadership Lesson #4 also alludes to asking for permission only when really necessary. Dey (n.d.) suggests that adults need to learn to trust themselves more and rely more on their own judgment. She notes that some people don't pursue their dreams because

> *They are waiting for someone to tell them that they have enough brains, talent or beauty to do whatever it is that they want to do. If you are waiting for someone to tell you to do something amazing with your life, you are going to be waiting a long time.… No one who has ever achieved anything great has gotten permission to do so. They simply have been bold and gone for it.*
> (para. 5)

It is true that many wonderful programs and initiatives became a reality only because no one asked permission first. It is also true that moving ahead without permission always carries some personal risk. But it's critical *not to ask for permission if "no" is not an option.*

It is also true that perception is a factor in determining whether permission is even needed. Schmidt (2017) suggests that rebellion often begins when someone thinks permission should not be requested for something considered a fundamental right. Perhaps that is why some leadership experts suggest it is far better to ask for forgiveness than to ask for permission. If your intentions are good and you see a problem that you have the skills and time to fix, then be willing to take the risks to do so. If things don't go well, ask for forgiveness. Own that failure, and learn from the consequences.

"On one side of the permission spectrum are people who feel their personal freedoms and potential are restricted by seeking permission. On the other side are the people who take ownership or responsibility for a person, object or situation."

—Maren Schmidt (2017, para. 3)

Perhaps Bradberry (2017, para. 16) says it best:

> *Fear is the number one source of regret. When all is said and done, you will lament the chances you didn't take far more than you will your failures. Don't be afraid to take risks. I often hear people say, "What's the worst thing that can happen to you? Will it kill you?" Yet, death isn't the worst thing that can happen to you—the worst thing that can happen to you is allowing yourself to die inside while you're still alive.*

REFERENCES

Anyado, O. (2015, May 27). Visionaries are leaders of distinction. *LinkedIn.* Retrieved from https://www.linkedin.com/pulse/visionaries-leaders-distinction-onyi-anyado

Bradberry, T. (2017, January 28). 10 harsh lessons that will make you more successful [Blog post]. Retrieved from http://www.huffingtonpost.com/dr-travis-bradberry/10-harsh-lessons-that-wil_b_14422346.html

Carton, A. (2017, March 16). Meaningful work: What leaders can learn from NASA and the space race. Wharton, University of Pennsylvania. Retrieved from http://knowledge.wharton.upenn.edu/article/what-leaders-can-learn-from-nasa/

Dey, M. (n.d.). Stop asking for permission. *BeliefNet.* Retrieved from http://www.beliefnet.com/columnists/yourmorningcupofinspiration/2016/06/stop-asking-for-permission.html

Heathfield, S. (2016, October 12). Leadership vision. *The Balance.* Retrieved from https://www.thebalance.com/leadership-vision-1918616

Hyatt, M. (2012, January 23). Why vision is more important than strategy [Blog post]. Retrieved from https://michaelhyatt.com/why-vision-is-more-important-than-strategy.html

Marquis, B., & Huston, C. (2017). *Leadership roles and management functions in nursing* (9th ed.). Philadelphia, PA: Wolters Kluwer.

Melnyk, B., Malloch, K., & Gallagher-Ford, L. (2017). Developing effective leaders to meet 21st century health care challenges. In C. Huston (Ed.), *Professional issues in nursing: Challenges and opportunities* (Chapter 3). Philadelphia, PA: Wolters Kluwer.

Quy, L. (2017, March 15). 10 hard skills to learn that will last a lifetime. SmartBrief. Retrieved from http://www.smartbrief.com/original/2017/03/10-hard-skills-learn-will-last-lifetime

Schmidt, M. (2017, January 7). Asking permission [Blog post]. Retrieved from http://marenschmidt.com/2017/01/asking-permission/

Zate, K. (2011, October 8). Steve Jobs & the importance of vision to leadership. *EyesOnSales*. Retrieved from http://www.eyesonsales.com/content/article/steve_jobs_the_importance_of_vision_to_leadership/

5

MAINTAIN PERSONAL POWER: KEEP GAS IN THE TANK AND MONEY IN THE BANK

Leadership Lesson #5 is about maneuverability and personal power. This lesson suggests that having *gas in the tank and money in the bank* will reduce the possibility of being taken for granted or abused by anyone. In other words, individuals with resources and flexibility have more choices regarding where they live, where they work, and what they do in their lives. When you feel like you have some control over your life and the choices you make, others are less likely to take advantage of you.

For example, financial resources are critical to maneuverability. You don't have to be wealthy to maintain some control; you just need to have enough money to allow yourself options. Even those who have relatively small salaries can choose how they live to create the financial cushion needed to be maneuverable. During the economic downturn, many people felt trapped in jobs because they had bills to pay and families to support, and they feared they couldn't find another job in a recessed job market. Wouldn't it be incredibly freeing to be able to make life decisions that aren't tied to your next paycheck?

Personal power, then, means having the ability to change the direction of your life if you want to do so (Pathway to Happiness, n.d.). Harper (n.d., para. 2) agrees, noting that "knowingly or not, many of us have given away our personal power (or part thereof) and allowed situations, circumstances, and other people to dictate, direct, and control our reality for far too long." In doing so, we give away our control, hope, and happiness.

"Money is important because it enables you to have more control over your life, more freedom to carve out your own path and less constraints on your choices. How many of us are stuck in a career or in a job we hate, but cannot afford to lose, because losing our job would mean losing our house and our health insurance?"

—Vered Deleeuw
(n.d., para. 9)

In fact, I often share a personal situation to bring this point home. At the time, I was a relatively new staff nurse working in a critical care unit of a hospital. Like many new nurses, I couldn't wait to put school behind me and start bringing home a paycheck to buy what I considered to be the nicer things in life. Within a few years, my husband and I were proudly sporting a new mortgage, a car payment, and a lifestyle that spent what we were making. He went back to school, and I was the primary breadwinner. I shared all these new things in our lives with the people I worked with. Little did I know that I would soon regret this.

After I had worked on the unit for about a year, the supervisor announced that someone would have to work rotating shifts for a few months to cover an RN who needed an extended medical leave. No one volunteered. At that point, my supervisor told me that I would be the one who had to work rotating shifts. When I objected and pointed out that there were newer employees than I, she said that they refused to do so, threatening to quit first. When I suggested I might also quit if forced to take on the assignment, she said, "*You* have a mortgage and a car and a husband in school. You can't afford to quit, so you'll do it."

The problem was that she was right, and I did work those rotating shifts. It was a valuable lesson for me—be careful how much personal information you share with your employer, or with anyone for that matter, about your lack of maneuverability, as it may ultimately be used against you.

"The truth is, each time you stand up for what's fair, you respect yourself. When you stop allowing others to take advantage of you and respect yourself, your self-esteem improves."

—Emily Roberts (2015, para. 2)

Unwittingly, I had enabled my employer to take advantage of me. I wasn't as maneuverable as I should have been, my employer knew it, and my options were limited as a result.

Unfortunately, many people fail to recognize the importance of personal power. We all need some degree of power to accomplish our goals as well as those shared with our followers. In addition, strong political skills, such as building connections, fostering trust, and influencing others, are essential qualities of a transformational leader (Brooks, 2016).

Unfortunately, however, many people mistrust power, particularly women. Being powerful is infinitely preferable to being powerless. In fact, most people dislike being powerless because everyone needs to feel as though they have some control over their lives.

I also disagree with the old adage "power corrupts." Instead, I believe that being powerless is more likely to corrupt. That's because when you have no real power, you tend to be bossy, create too many rules, and become rigid in your decision-making so you at least *appear* powerful. In contrast, truly powerful people know that they are powerful and don't need to visibly show that power.

"POWERLESS NURSES ARE INEFFECTIVE NURSES."

—Annie Thakore (2015, para. 1)

Individuals can do many things to increase their maneuverability and personal power. Getting an education is one. Having knowledge and skill that others lack increases an individual's personal power base. The 2010 Institute of Medicine (IOM) report *The Future of Nursing: Leading Change, Advancing Health* calls for an 80% baccalaureate-prepared nursing workforce and a doubling of doctorates held by nurses by 2020 (Robert Wood Johnson Foundation, 2013). The report notes that higher degrees in nursing yield significant benefits for patients, employers, and communities. Nurses with higher education also have more career options, including management roles, advanced practice roles, and emerging jobs in telemedicine, nurse navigation, and informatics.

Higher degrees in nursing also mean higher salaries. PayScale (2017) notes that in 2017, the annual salary range for a female nurse with a master's degree (MSN) was $64,925 to $101,538, with males making $73,923 to $113,965. Salaries in some states—such as California, Pennsylvania, and New York—were much higher.

Even specialty certifications can increase personal power and maneuverability. To achieve professional certification, nurses must meet eligibility criteria that may include years and types of work experience as well as minimum educational levels, active nursing licenses, and successful completion of a nationally administered examination. Benefits of certification may include more rapid promotions on career ladders, advancement opportunities, and feelings of accomplishment. In addition, certified nurses often earn more than their noncertified counterparts (Huston, 2017).

Another strategy for increasing personal power is to maintain high energy levels. Power and energy go hand in hand:

> *Effective leaders take sufficient time to unwind, reflect, rest, and have fun when they feel tired. Taking time for significant relationships and developing outside interests are important so that other resources are available for sustenance when political forces in the organization drain energy. (Marquis & Huston, 2017, p. 334)*

Eblin (2017) agrees, noting that individuals are better poised to manage their stress and perform at their best when they take care of their health and well-being. This includes moving throughout the day, being intentional about eating moderate amounts of healthy food, and getting at least 7 hours of sleep at night.

"YOU MUST TAKE CARE OF YOURSELF BEFORE YOU CAN TAKE CARE OF OTHERS."

—Bessie Marquis and Carol Huston (2017, p. 334)

Presenting a positive image to others is also important in maintaining personal power. Marquis and Huston (2017, p. 334) note that how people look, act, and talk influence whether others view them as powerful or powerless:

> *The nurse who stands tall and is poised, assertive, articulate, and well-groomed presents a picture of personal control and power. The person who looks like a victim will undoubtedly become one. When individuals take the time for self-care, they exude confidence. This is apparent in not only how they dress and act but also in how they interact with others.*

Developing a broader network is also a personal power-building strategy. Morgan (2016) notes that many employees interface solely with people in their own department, failing to get a broader view of the organization and the world around them. Having a broader perspective can lead to more strategic ideas and allow an individual to be a connector among the organization, the outside world, and the industry.

REFERENCES

Brooks, C. (2016, October 6). Want to be a better leader? Build your political skills. *Business News Daily*. Retrieved from http://www.businessnewsdaily.com/9465-political-skills-happiness.html

Deleeuw, V. (n.d.). Can we agree that money is important? *MoneyNing*. Retrieved from http://moneyning.com/money-beliefs/can-we-agree-that-money-is-important/

Eblin, S. (2017, January 19). The ten behaviors of strong personal leadership [Blog post]. Retrieved from https://eblingroup.com/blog/the-ten-behaviors-of-strong-personal-leadership

Harper, C. (n.d.). Take back your personal power (part 1). *Lifehack*. Retrieved from http://www.lifehack.org/articles/featured/take-back-your-personal-power-part-1.html

Huston, C. (2017). *Professional issues in nursing: Challenges and opportunities* (4th ed.). Philadelphia, PA: Wolters Kluwer.

Marquis, B., & Huston, C. (2017). *Leadership roles and management functions in nursing* (9th ed.). Philadelphia, PA: Wolters Kluwer.

Morgan, J. (2016, September 28). Act like a leader, think like a leader: How to change the course of your career. *Inc.* Retrieved from https://www.inc.com/jacob-morgan/act-like-a-leader-think-like-a-leader-how-to-change-the-course-of-your-career.html

Pathway to Happiness. (n.d.). Developing personal power. Retrieved from http://www.pathwaytohappiness.com/personal-power.htm

PayScale. (2017). Master of science in nursing (MSN) degree average salary. Retrieved from http://www.payscale.com/research/US/Degree=Master_of_Science_in_Nursing_(MSN)/Salary

Robert Wood Johnson Foundation. (2013, September). Charting nursing's future. Reports on policies that can transform patient care. Issue 21. Retrieved from http://www.rwjf.org/content/dam/farm/reports/issue_briefs/2013/rwjf407597

Roberts, E. (2015, April 3). Respect yourself: Stop letting others take advantage of you [Blog post]. Retrieved from https://www.healthyplace.com/blogs/buildingselfesteem/2015/04/respect-yourself-stop-letting-others-take-advantage-of-you/

Thakore, A. (2015, May 27). Empowering nurses..why is it essential?? *LinkedIn*. Retrieved from https://www.linkedin.com/pulse/empowering-nurseswhy-essential-dr-annie-thakore

6

CHOOSE YOUR BATTLES CAREFULLY

eadership Lesson #6 is choose your battles carefully. Sometimes we spend a lot of time and effort trying to make obnoxious people happy, but they will never be happy! Not everyone will like you as a leader. Accept those who do and move on. Bradberry (2017b) agrees that not everyone will support you. In fact, he suggests that most people will not.

Sometimes, though, this is hard to do. I'm sure we can all think of a situation or two where some truly obnoxious person was able to bring us down to his or her level. The problem is that these individuals are likely much better at bullying than you, because they've had more practice. And when you try to compete with a bully, you're probably going to lose.

That brings me back to a situation where I learned this lesson the hard way. I was a staff nurse in the ICU. One of the local vascular surgeons, whom I'll call Dr. X, had a quick temper and a history of bullying nurses. His policy was that postoperative patients with a temperature of 37.4 degrees C or higher needed nasotracheal (NT) suctioning to keep their lungs clear. Because NT suctioning was so traumatic to patients, the nurses often tried some basic cooling measures first.

On this particular day, I finished morning handoff and went in to check on one of my patients who was recovering uneventfully from a femoral artery bypass. He was under numerous blankets, and when I checked his temperature, it was 37.4 degrees C. I informed the patient that I was going to

"Some people will inundate you with negativity, passive aggression, anger, or jealousy, but none of this matters, because, as Dr. Seuss said, 'Those that matter don't mind, and those that mind don't matter.' We can't possibly get support from everyone, and we definitely can't spend our time and energy trying to win over the people who don't support us. Letting go of the opinions of people who don't matter frees up time and energy for the people and things that do."

—Travis Bradberry (2017b, para. 14)

take off a few blankets and let him wake up, and then I would recheck his temperature. Just then, I turned around and saw Dr. X standing behind me. He moved to within inches of my face and began screaming at the top of his voice, asking whether I thought this patient looked like a lizard. I was more than a little confused. I was also embarrassed, because every nurse in the unit was watching the interaction. Even the patients in other cubicles were trying to see what was going on.

When I asked Dr. X what he meant about the patient looking like a lizard, he began yelling that the patient was not a cold-blooded animal that would adapt his temperature to his surroundings. My normal response would have been to try to collaborate with this doctor or at least to be respectful. But that day, I just got mad. Everyone was watching, and I was embarrassed. I did the worst possible thing to do with a bully: I tried to compete. I responded, "So tell me, Dr. X, why does a cooling blanket work?"

As you can imagine, Dr. X exploded. In fact, I think the whole unit shook! He was so angry that he was trembling. He immediately left the unit and went to see the Director of Nursing, demanding that I be fired. The phone rang several minutes later, and I was summoned to the nursing office for a chat. In the end, I was not fired. In fact, the nursing supervisor was very understanding—although she did ask me to really think about what I would do differently the next time to keep a situation like this from escalating.

One of the most important leadership lessons I learned from this situation was not to compete with a bully unless you absolutely have to. When someone "shoots angry at us, we sense it and instinctively throw it back at them. When this happens, we hook into their energy" (Pearson, 2010, para. 9). Try stepping back to pause and reflect on what has occurred so that you can gain control of your negative emotions. The ability to manage your emotions and remain calm under pressure is part of emotional intelligence and effective leadership (Bradberry, 2017a). The reality is that you likely can't control the bully's behavior, but you *can* control your response and learn to react in a way that allows you to move forward.

"TalentSmart conducted research with more than a million people, and found that 90% of top performers are skilled at managing their emotions in times of stress in order to remain calm and in control. One of their greatest gifts is the ability to identify toxic people and keep them at bay."

—Travis Bradberry (2017a, para. 19)

A second leadership lesson I learned was that if you are going to compete with a bully, don't do it in front of your patients. And finally, while fighting back did give me a momentary thrill, the result was that in doing so, I brought myself down to his level and gave up some of my own power. I must admit, though, I never had any trouble with him from that point on.

Whitbourne (2015) suggests that, when confronted by an obnoxious person, you first step back and attempt to understand the source of your annoyance. Is the behavior truly obnoxious, or are you responding to it with anger because it hits upon your insecurities? Secondly, she recommends that you try to ignore the obnoxious behavior if possible. Many people who behave in obnoxious ways do so to get attention, and the behavior may diminish if you don't give them that reinforcement.

At other times, however, Whitbourne (2015) notes that the individual causing the turmoil must be directly confronted. The confrontation sometimes needs to come from a person other than the target of the bullying. Involving your manager or someone with formal authority may be necessary, and incidents should be documented if they are repetitive. It is also important in confrontation to allow the offender to preserve some self-esteem if possible, or the conflict aftermath may be even greater than the original conflict. Dachis (2013, para. 12) agrees, suggesting that you shouldn't fight any battle if you can't do so constructively and stay solution-focused: "If your goal is to hurt or just express your anger, you're fighting for the wrong reasons. Every single argument you have ought to aim to improve an undesirable situation."

The bottom line, though, is that all nurses must recognize that verbal abuse, incivility, and bullying are not simply part of the job. Bad behavior cannot be perpetually ignored. Nurses must stand up and defend themselves. Brunt (2015) notes that nurses and students need to be given information on how to address conflicts and change disruptive behavior in the workplace so that nurses, individually and collectively, can eliminate bullying and workplace violence.

"CIVILITY COSTS NOTHING AND BUYS EVERYTHING."

—Mary Wortley Montagu
(as cited in BrainyQuote, n.d.)

"A lot of cheap seats in the arena are filled with people who never venture onto the floor. They just hurl mean-spirited criticisms and put-downs from a safe distance. The problem is, when we stop caring what people think and stop feeling hurt by cruelty, we lose our ability to connect. But when we're defined by what people think, we lose the courage to be vulnerable. Therefore, we need to be selective about the feedback we let into our lives."

—Brené Brown, *Rising Strong* (as cited in Lammersen, 2017, para. 10)

REFERENCES

Bradberry, T. (2017a, January 2). 6 toxic bosses you should avoid like the plague [Blog post]. Retrieved from http://www.huffingtonpost.com/dr-travis-bradberry/6-toxic-bosses-you-should_b_13772058.html

Bradberry, T. (2017b, January 28). 10 harsh lessons that will make you more successful [Blog post]. Retrieved from http://www.huffingtonpost.com/dr-travis-bradberry/10-harsh-lessons-that-wil_b_14422346.html

BrainyQuote. (n.d.). Mary Wortley Montagu quotes. Retrieved from https://www.brainyquote.com/quotes/authors/m/mary_wortley_montagu.html quotes/authors/m/mary_wortley_montagu.html

Brooks, C. (2016, October 6). Want to be a better leader? Build your political skills. *Business News Daily*. Retrieved from http://www.businessnewsdaily.com/9465-political-skills-happiness.html

Brunt, B. (2015). Breaking the cycle of horizontal violence. *Ohio Nurses Review, 8*(3), 12–15.

Dachis, A. (2013, March 11). How to choose your battles and fight for what actually matters. *Lifehacker*. Retrieved from http://lifehacker.com/5989295/how-to-choose-your-battles-and-fight-for-what-actually-matters

Lammersen, R. (2017, January 10). Here's to the swimmers & the spectators: A lesson in vulnerability [Blog post]. Retrieved from http://www.huffingtonpost.com/rebecca-lammersen/heres-to-the-swimmers-the_b_14085696.html

Pearson, A. (2010, July 19). 10 tips for dealing with annoying people. *Bloom Life Design*. Retrieved from http://www.bloomlifedesign.com/10-tips-for-dealing-with-annoying-people/

Whitbourne, S. K. (2015, May 19). 4 ways to deal with obnoxious people. *Psychology Today*. Retrieved from https://www.psychologytoday.com/blog/fulfillment-any-age/201505/4-ways-deal-obnoxious-people

7

PERFECT THE "ART" OF COMMUNICATION

eadership Lesson #7 is the vital role of expert communication skills in achieving success as a leader. Most of us have heard about the importance of well-developed communication skills so many times that we take them for granted. Yet the ability to communicate effectively is one of the most underrated leadership skills.

Surdek (2017) agrees, noting that leaders don't always realize the impact of their language when talking with their teams. You can do many things with language, from empowering people to generating new possibilities. Indeed, Myatt (2012) suggests that if you examine the world's greatest leaders, you will find that all are exceptional communicators. That's because they talk about their ideas in a way that speaks to the emotions and aspirations of others. They also realize that if their message "does not take deep root with the audience then it likely won't be understood, much less championed" (para. 2).

So what makes someone a great orator? Greene (2014) says that for John F. Kennedy (JFK), it was passion and authenticity; a voice tone that included variation in pace (sometimes fast, sometimes slow) as well as variation in volume (sometimes loud, sometimes soft) and pitch; great vocal punctuation and dramatic, yet natural, pauses; body language that was warm and accessible, strong and determined, yet playful and relaxed, all at the right time; and finally—a laser compelling message. JFK's speeches also built on *ethos*, the notion that identifying with the values and beliefs of the audience creates a sense of community and trust (Glover, 2011).

> "MOST LEADERS UNDERSTAND THE CONSEQUENCES OF POOR FINANCIAL MANAGEMENT; BUT NOT ALL LEADERS APPRECIATE THE IMPORTANCE OF COMMUNICATION SKILLS FOR LEADERSHIP AND MANAGEMENT."

—Phillip Decker and Jordan Mitchell (2017, para. 8)

For Martin Luther King Jr. (MLK), it was authenticity (his life was consistent with his rhetoric), and his emotion emerged naturally from his genuinely intense belief in his message. MLK also used vivid illustrations that business and professional leaders could relate to easily as well as simple, clear, language—forming catchy, attention-riveting word contrasts and combinations (Lampton, n.d.). In addition, his message sustained magnetism, because his theme was consistent and unwavering.

MLK also employed metaphors: He used "my dream" to stand for a much larger vision of the future. He also brought in the element of *pathos*, suggesting that he might not live long enough to see that future, which brought his audience closer to him emotionally (Glover, 2011).

The ability to use vivid illustrations, coin creative words and phrases, use classical techniques that emphasize logic and lyrical rhythm, and deliver believable messages with charisma and conviction is an "art." Exceptional speakers leave listeners wanting more. For most of us, becoming a powerful orator is a long-term goal—gaining these skills takes a great deal of work and practice as well as some natural ability. But being a truly great communicator requires much more than just writing and speaking articulately.

Communicating is also listening, an art that is talked about a lot but much harder to do in real life. Indeed, Holmes (2015) notes that the average person listens with only 25% efficiency—which means we miss a lot of messages. Why don't we listen? Sometimes it's because we think we already know what someone is going to say. This is especially true when we think something is obvious, even when it is not. Sometimes we fail to listen because we are busy trying to multitask, and our attention is divided.

Like becoming a great orator, becoming a good listener is a learned skill. Unfortunately, listening is the most valuable skill nobody teaches (Maltoni, 2017). Maltoni argues that because this activity happens in the mind, we need to be actively involved in the process. Otherwise, we're just hearing.

Contrary to common assumption, when we're listening, we should not be passive, like receivers; our participation is required for comprehension.

Thus, active listening must be practiced. Being mindful in conversations, keeping an open mind, not interrupting, and eliminating distractions can help. To become an active listener, Cook (2017) suggests pretending you are on the television program *Shark Tank*. Entrepreneurs on *Shark Tank* stop talking almost immediately when a Shark starts to speak. With a lot at stake, the entrepreneurs pay attention to the new ways they need to behave to get what they want.

In addition, Marquis and Huston (2017) suggest that to become better listeners, leaders must first understand how their own experiences, values, attitudes, and biases affect how they receive and perceive messages. Second, they must overcome information and communication overload. It is easy to stop listening actively when you are overwhelmed. The leader's primary purpose is to receive the message being sent rather than to form a response before the transmission of the message is complete.

McKay (2017) says it's also important to maintain eye contact and nod your head to indicate to the speaker that you are taking in the information he or she is conveying. Also, be attentive to nonverbal cues, such as facial expressions and posture, to get the full gist of what the speaker is saying, and ask appropriate questions. Remember that nonverbal communication speaks more loudly than verbal communication, especially when the messages are not congruent.

"IT IS SIMPLY IMPOSSIBLE TO BECOME A GREAT LEADER WITHOUT BEING A GREAT COMMUNICATOR. I HOPE YOU NOTICED THE PREVIOUS SENTENCE DIDN'T REFER TO BEING A GREAT TALKER—BIG DIFFERENCE."

—Mike Myatt (2012, para. 1)

"WISDOM IS THE REWARD YOU GET FOR A LIFETIME OF LISTENING WHEN YOU'D HAVE PREFERRED TO TALK."

—Doug Larson (as cited in Goodreads, 2017, para. 1)

We also need to be careful *how* we communicate. Some things are too important to communicate via letter or email. When you talk to people face to face, they have the opportunity to validate that they heard or to ask questions.

In addition, Myatt (2012) reminds us not to assume someone is ready to have a specific conversation just because we're ready. Leaders often must pave the way for productive conversations. In addition, leaders don't assume that people know where they are coming from, if they haven't told them what their objectives are.

Leaders also need to be sensitive regarding whom they communicate with, what the message is, and how it should best be communicated. Truly smart leaders will keep lines of communication open with their followers and repeat important messages multiple times, in multiple formats, until they are sure the messages have been heard and interpreted correctly.

Communication is complex, and so many things can interfere with the messages we are trying to send. For example, status, power, and authority can be barriers to communication. In addition, "Too much information, poorly framed messages, inappropriate channels, and incomplete feedback from the recipient to the sender on how well the message is understood and accepted can all be self-handicapping. It is the leader's responsibility to ensure that all take place effectively" (Decker & Mitchell, 2017, para. 11).

REFERENCES

Cook, K. (2017, March 14). 9 strategies for becoming a super-communicator. *The Business Journals*. Retrieved from http://www.bizjournals.com/bizjournals/how-to/growth-strategies/2017/03/9-strategies-for-becoming-a-super-communicator.html

Decker, P., & Mitchell, J. (2017, January 5). Importance of communication skills for leadership and management. *Manage Magazine*. Retrieved from https://managemagazine.com/article-bank/self-handicapping-leadership/importance-communication-skills-leadership-management/

Glover, D. (2011). *The art of great speeches: And why we remember them*. Cambridge, UK: Cambridge University Press.

Goodreads Inc. (2017). Doug Larson quotes. Retrieved from https://www.goodreads.com/author/quotes/4341759.Doug_Larson

Greene, R. (2014, November 21). The 7 reasons why JFK is one of the world's greatest speakers, and what we can learn from him [Blog post]. Retrieved from http://www.huffingtonpost.com/richard-greene/the-7-reasons-why-jfk-is-_b_6200548.html

Holmes, L. (2015, May 20). 9 things good listeners do differently [Blog post]. Retrieved from http://www.huffingtonpost.com/2014/08/14/habits-of-good-listeners_n_5668590.html

Lampton, B. (n.d.). Dr. Martin Luther King, Jr.—Role model for speaking. *Business Know-How*. Retrieved from http://www.businessknowhow.com/growth/mlk.htm

Maltoni, V. (2017, February 1). We can only listen once. *Conversation Agent*. Retrieved from http://www.conversationagent.com/2017/01/how-to-listen.html

Marquis, B., & Huston, C. (2017). *Leadership roles and management functions in nursing* (9th ed.). Philadelphia, PA: Wolters Kluwer.

McKay, D. M. (2017, March 6). Why you need excellent listening skills. *The Balance*. Retrieved from https://www.thebalance.com/listening-skills-524853

Myatt, M. (2012, April 4). 10 communication secrets of great leaders. *Forbes*. Retrieved from https://www.forbes.com/sites/mikemyatt/2012/04/04/10-communication-secrets-of-great-leaders/#6745be4422fe

Surdek, S. (2017, February 7). How to engage your team by using the right communication. *Forbes*. Retrieved from https://www.forbes.com/sites/forbescoachescouncil/2017/02/07/how-to-engage-your-team-by-using-the-right-language/#ce5486874e05

8

APPRECIATE AND EMPOWER FOLLOWERS

Leadership Lesson #8 is to appreciate and empower followers, an underappreciated factor in the leadership equation. Good followers make leadership look easy, and a leader often overlooks how followers contribute to the leader's success. "Everyone wants to feel that they count for something and are important to someone. People will work harder, and work more, for those who care about them, and their trust will earn you respect" (Daskal, 2015, para. 7).

Showing appreciation can be as simple as saying thank you when someone does something for you, big or little.

> *Most of us really do want to be thanked for the things that we do, even if it's something that we're supposed to be doing anyway. Being appreciated is one of those things that really motivates us, both at work and in life, so a little goes a long way if you can offer up a genuine thank you when it's appropriate. (Laura Trice, as cited in Henry, 2014, para. 2)*

Recognition should also be as immediate as possible. Praise becomes less effective as a motivational tool as the time between the action taken and the recognition increases.

"Successful leaders understand the nature of teams and their role on a team. The effective leader, when working on a team, understands that the leader's goal is for the team to be successful. The effective leader knows that to be successful, each person must relinquish his or her own agenda for personal success and embrace the opportunity to share success with the team."

—Bernadette Melnyk, Kathy Malloch, and Lynn Gallagher-Ford (2017, p. 36)

In addition, giving praise and recognition may be even more meaningful when done in front of others. The old adage to "praise in public and criticize in private" has merit, because public praise encourages other followers to replicate the behavior that earned the praise. Zak (2017) agrees, suggesting that recognition is most powerful for both the colleague being recognized and others in the organization when it:

» Is based on meeting a stretch goal

» Occurs within a week of the goal's being reached

» Is personal, public, tangible, and unexpected

» Comes from peers

This can vary, though, among followers, as some people are embarrassed by public recognition. And, it may evoke feelings of jealousy in those who were not recognized for their accomplishments in the past.

When showing appreciation, being specific is also important (Maroney, 2015). Vague praise sounds insincere. Instead of just saying, "I really am grateful for the good job you do around here," you might say, "I really appreciate how you dealt with the agitated patient last night. Your efforts kept a volatile situation from getting out of control." When you are specific, followers realize that you are truly watching their actions and recognize their unique contributions (Maroney, 2015).

Biro (2015, para. 2) cautions, however, that we have become a society "in which people expect to be rewarded for drawing breath and taking up space," which makes meaningful recognition difficult. If many of your followers expect routine and social praise, how can you recognize extraordinary achievement? Biro suggests that you avoid constant praise for average work and remember that recognition can be a key tool in motivating followers only when it recognizes extra effort and is authentic, not automatic. Praising for the sake of praising is meaningless; it must be genuine and come from the heart. Otherwise, it is just flattery.

In addition, followers feel appreciated when they are empowered. This requires leaders to guide followers and lead from the bottom up rather than the top down. Greenleaf (1977) calls this *servant leadership*. The basic premise of servant leadership is that the leader's first aim is to serve and help followers fulfill their roles so followers can grow and progress (Northouse, 2016).

Servant leaders put serving others, including employees, customers, and the community, as the Number 1 priority. Thus, servant leaders are more concerned with the needs of others than their own needs, and they lead through their service. In addition, servant leaders foster a service inclination in others that promotes collaboration, teamwork, and collective activism. Thus, followers help not only themselves but the organizations where they work and contribute. Indeed, extensive research has shown that organizations whose leaders establish caring cultures achieve substantially higher performance (Zak, 2017).

Daskal (2015) agrees, noting that when you groom others, you transfer authority to them. You allow them to share in the load and give them opportunity to lead. In empowering others, you're ultimately working toward the day when they can lead their own followers. Indeed, nothing should be as rewarding to a leader as when their followers feel empowered enough to take on leadership roles. It's like being a parent. You know you've done a

"LEADERSHIP IS SERVICE, NOT POSITION."

—Tim Fargo (as cited in McMahon, 2017, para. 2)

"WHEN YOU EMPOWER PEOPLE, YOU'RE INFLUENCING NOT ONLY THEM, BUT ALSO ALL THE PEOPLE THEY WILL INFLUENCE IN TURN THROUGH THEIR LEADERSHIP. THAT IS EMPOWERING."

—Lolly Daskal (2015, para. 13)

good job when your children can independently leave home and begin new lives. The same is true when your followers go on to become leaders.

In empowering followers, however, the leader must remember that some of the execution decisions followers make will fail. Zak (2017, para. 10) notes that an important part of a leader's job is to

> *Help people correct mistakes and to sustain risk-management backstops so failures are not catastrophic. When coaching subordinates is done with genuine care for them, trust increases and performance improves. This means treating others as full human beings, with imperfections, emotions, and a personal life, not as replaceable human capital.*

According to Marcus (2017, para. 2), leaders must also take special note of those quiet followers who often "lead from the back of the room." Marcus notes that these individuals often embody the soul of the effort and emerge as the glue that binds. "They may not be the most authoritative or the jump starter, but they will be the anchor. They will be your closer—the person who moves your effort across the finish line" (para. 3).

In addition, it is not just the leader who sets the agenda or determines priorities for action. It's like an iceberg. The iceberg (leader) seen above the water is the most obvious, but it is the support of the followers (the mass under the water) that really makes the difference in the power of the iceberg. Schwarz

(2016) suggests that too many people still believe that the essence of leadership is about influencing others to do what we want them to do. Instead, Schwarz says that you must be genuinely open to being influenced by others. Otherwise, any leadership approach you use that relies on your team's collective knowledge is likely to fail. Smart leaders are in touch with the needs and wants of their followers and build teams to achieve a shared purpose.

Finally, smart leaders will remember that although followers must be appreciated and empowered, they may influence leaders in negative ways. For example, followers can and do mislead leaders, whether intentionally or not. We can all think of situations where we have been misled with biased or incomplete information. In addition, leaders sometimes find it hard to differentiate between friends and enemies. It is true that you want to hold your enemies as close as your friends. It's equally true that being a leader will likely win you some false friends as well as some true enemies.

Remember that sometimes it's hard as a leader to figure out whom you can trust. But trust is the cornerstone between leaders and followers, and it's very difficult to lead if you can't trust that your followers are right there behind you.

"LEADERSHIP IS NOT A 'SOLO ACT'; IT IS IMBEDDED IN RELATIONSHIPS, EFFECTIVE COMMUNICATION, SHARED OWNERSHIP, AND COACHING AND MOTIVATING OTHERS."

—Bernadette Melnyk, Kathy Malloch, and Lynn Gallagher-Ford (2017, p. 29)

REFERENCES

Biro, M. M. (2015, December 8). 5 ways leaders rock employee recognition. *TalentCulture*. Retrieved from http://www.talentculture.com/5-ways-leaders-rock-employee-recognition/

Daskal, L. (2015). The act of empowering others changes lives [Blog post]. Retrieved from http://www.lollydaskal.com/leadership/the-act-of-empowering-others-changes-lives/

Evans, L. (2015, August 26). Why saying "thank you" is more important than giving employees a raise. *Entrepreneur*. Retrieved from https://www.entrepreneur.com/article/249933

Greenleaf, R. K. (1977). *Servant leadership: A journey in the nature of legitimate power and greatness*. New York, NY: Paulist.

Henry, A. (2014, April 17). The importance of saying thank you, and why you should say it often. *Lifehacker*. Retrieved from http://lifehacker.com/the-importance-of-saying-thank-you-and-why-you-should-1563980468

Marcus, I. (2017, March 2). Empowering the quiet team leader. *Great Leadership*. Retrieved from http://www.greatleadershipbydan.com/2017/03/empowering-quiet-team-leader.html

Maroney, J. P. (2015, February 20). Four pillars of employee motivation—February 20, 2015. *PPAI Publications*. Retrieved from http://pubs.ppai.org/2015/02/four-pillars-of-employee-motivation-february-20-2015/

McMahon, T. (2017, February 24). Lean quote: Leadership is service, not position [Blog post]. Retrieved from http://www.aleanjourney.com/2017/02/lean-quote-leadership-is-service-not.html

Melnyk, B., Malloch, K., & Gallagher-Ford, L. (2017). Developing effective leaders to meet 21st century health care challenges. In C. Huston (Ed.), *Professional issues in nursing: Challenges and opportunities* (Chapter 3). Philadelphia, PA: Wolters Kluwer.

Northouse, P. G. (2016). *Leadership: Theory and practice* (7th ed.). Thousand Oaks, CA: SAGE.

Schwarz, R. (2016, August 24). How leaders can help others influence them. *Harvard Business Review.* Retrieved from https://hbr.org/2016/08/how-leaders-can-help-others-influence-them

Zak, P. J. (2017, March 17). How to be a trusted leader. *CEO.* Retrieved from http://blogs.the-ceo-magazine.com/guest/how-be-trusted-leader

9

SET
PRIORITIES
AND ENJOY
THE
JOURNEY

Leadership Lesson #9 is to set priorities and enjoy the journey. We should spend our time on what is most important to us. We all have some control over our life priorities, yet we often feel that too much of our time and energy is directed toward meeting the priorities of others. When that is the case, life becomes a stressful series of tasks to do and deadlines to meet, and we forget to appreciate the successes and joy encountered on the journey itself.

When people focus solely on the destination and not the journey, they put off *what really matters* in pursuit of things they want to achieve, and they tell themselves that they'll worry about those things once they've reached their destination (Noé, n.d.). Few of us have already accomplished everything in life that we want to. In fact, the truth is: "No matter how much you achieve, accomplish, and acquire in life … there is always something more to be had. You'll never 'reach' your final destination—at least not in this life!" (para. 3). The key is finding the right balance and discovering a mind-set that allows us to pursue big things without sacrificing the *"little things"* that make life worth living (para. 6).

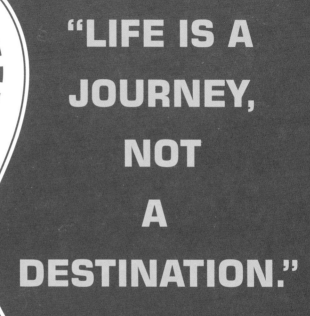

"LIFE IS A JOURNEY, NOT A DESTINATION."

—Ralph Waldo Emerson
(as cited in Goodreads,
2017, para. 1)

One of my favorite instructors in my doctoral program surprised me on the first day of classes by reminding us that the world didn't begin and end with coming back to school and earning an advanced degree. He repeatedly told us to eat more hot fudge sundaes, have more picnics, eat more potato salad, and take more walks in the park. He also said to make sure we slow down enough to enjoy the journey. Sometimes we are so busy racing from one event to another, or flying from one emotion to another, that we just stop being present.

I've often thought about his advice, and I think he was right. Slowing down enough to appreciate life's great moments is an ongoing challenge. Having a life filled with new opportunities for learning and growing, though, is part of what makes the journey worthwhile to me. I love new challenges and new opportunities to contribute to the world in some meaningful way. I love having the opportunity to be a leader in nursing, and I love traveling around the world, meeting other nurses, and feeling like I am making a difference in my profession.

But the leadership journey each of you may choose to pursue will likely be very different. In fact, that's the wonderful thing about being both a nurse and a leader: We don't have to look alike, think alike, or want the same things. We can all be unique. What we do share in being a leader is the potential to positively influence others and the life journeys they embark upon. Indeed, I often think we discount the impact we can have on others' lives.

"INSTEAD OF LIVING IN THE LAND OF 'I COULD'VE, SHOULD'VE, WOULD'VE' OR 'WHAT IF,' TRY LIVING IN THE LAND OF 'I AM,' BECAUSE NOW IS THE ONLY MOMENT YOU CAN AFFECT AND ENJOY."

—Debbie Gisonni (2013, para. 4)

"PRIORITY SETTING IS PERHAPS THE MOST CRITICAL SKILL IN GOOD TIME MANAGEMENT, BECAUSE ALL ACTIONS WE TAKE HAVE SOME TYPE OF RELATIVE IMPORTANCE."

—Bessie Marquis and Carol Huston (2017, p. 214)

I still have students who come back 10 or 20 years later and tell me that I changed their life by a story I shared in class or a conversation I had with them. That's very powerful.

Time is likely our most precious resource, so learning to use it wisely is critical to achieving life goals. There are many competitors for our time and energy. For most of us, priorities include having positive and healthy relationships with our families and friends. We also need to pursue outside interests and hobbies and find time to work out, read, relax, and take great vacations—because power and energy *do* go hand in hand.

Sometimes, though, other people in our lives try to make their priorities our priorities. When this occurs, step back and ask whether meeting this priority or deadline is important, whether it is more important than our own priorities, and what the costs will be in meeting their priorities. Saying "no" is something we talk about frequently but don't do enough. Lidow (2017, para. 1) agrees, noting that smart leaders must identify trade-offs and choose what *not* to do as much as what *to* do: "Grading the importance of various initiatives in an environment of finite resources is a primary test of leadership."

In determining whether to do something, Lidow (2017) suggests it may be helpful to prioritize the request into one of three categories: critical, important, and desirable. A *critical* priority is an objective that must be successfully accomplished within a specified amount of time, no matter what.

An *important* priority, on the other hand, is an effort that can have a significant positive impact on performance. For these initiatives, resources are fixed, and the variable is either time or the objective. A *desirable* priority is an effort in which both resources and time are variables. Once the category is determined, it becomes easier to identify the appropriate objectives, resources, and time for each request or to simply refuse the request.

Marquis and Huston (2017) suggest an even simpler way of prioritizing what needs to be accomplished. Divide all requests into three categories: "don't do," "do later," and "do now." The "don't do" items probably reflect problems that will take care of themselves, are already outdated, or are better accomplished by someone else. The "do later" items can be set aside temporarily but should be broken down first into smaller projects with a specific timeline and plan for implementation. The "do now" items are important, and energy, attention, and resources should be committed to their timely completion.

It is also important to remember that not everything worth doing must be done to the highest level possible. Some things are just worth getting done, and other things must be done well or extremely well. Sometimes we seek a level of perfection in a task that isn't necessary as a way of avoiding what really needs to be done. Having clearly identified priorities can help you make this distinction.

Work is also an important part of who we are, especially when it is part of a thoughtfully chosen and carefully implemented career path. Having a career strategy, then, is important in managing the direction you want your career to take, the job skills and knowledge you will need, and how you can get them (Victoria, n.d.).

Having a vision and carefully articulated professional goals is an important part of your career strategy. Santaguida (2016, para. 3) notes:

> *This can be difficult for leaders, especially females, who worry about being pegged as overly ambitious, but let's be clear—there is nothing wrong with ambition. If you're not letting your managers and your company know where you want to go, chances are you'll never get there.*

"Few people ascend to leadership positions by accident, and achieving one's goals isn't something that just happens. Navigating your career takes more than a little ambition and good old-fashioned hard work—you have to know who you are and what you want, and you need to develop a clear roadmap for getting it."

—Kerri-Ann Santaguida (2016, para. 1)

You also need to have a specific plan for how you will achieve your career vision, with short- and long-term goals as well as timelines, because goals without a specific plan for completion rarely become a reality.

This doesn't mean, though, that life is not filled with obstacles and challenges. Being a nurse leader is fraught with complexity. There are wicked problems to solve, ongoing challenges of how best to balance the art and science of nursing, and perpetual needs to do more with less in almost every aspect of life. But as a leader, you have the skills you need to take on these challenges. You just need to have the confidence that the world is your oyster and that almost everything you want to achieve can be yours, if you plan and work toward it.

Be confident in who you are as a leader and what you have to share with others. Embrace the role, and make a difference in your profession. Our background and circumstances may have influenced who we are, but we are responsible for who we become.

Finally, remember my nine leadership lessons to help you on your leadership journey.

9 LEADERSHIP LESSONS

1 Find a Mentor and Positive Role Models to Share Your Journey

2 Be Self-Aware and Authentic

3 Be Able to Laugh at Yourself and Leave Your Ego at Home in a Jar

4 Be Visionary, Take Risks, and Ask for Permission Only When Necessary

5 Maintain Personal Power: Keep Gas in the Tank and Money in the Bank

6 Choose Your Battles Carefully

7 Perfect the "Art" of Communication

8 Appreciate and Empower Followers

9 Set Priorities and Enjoy the Journey

References

Gisonni, D. (2013, December 28). Live in the present and enjoy the journey of life [Blog post]. Retrieved from http://www.huffingtonpost.com/debbie-gisonni/live-in-the-present_b_4166290.html

Goodreads Inc. (2017). Ralph Waldo Emerson quotes. Retrieved from http://www.goodreads.com/quotes/24142-life-is-a-journey-not-a-destination

Lidow, D. (2017, February 13). A better way to set strategic priorities. *Harvard Business Review*. Retrieved from https://hbr.org/2017/02/a-better-way-to-set-strategic-priorities

Marquis, B., & Huston, C. (2017). *Leadership roles and management functions in nursing* (9th ed.). Philadelphia, PA: Wolters Kluwer.

Noé, K. (n.d.). It's all about the journey, not the destination. *Beliefnet*. Retrieved from http://www.beliefnet.com/inspiration/articles/its-all-about-the-journey-not-the-destination.aspx

Santaguida, K-A. (2016, August 23). How to navigate your career with intent. *The Globe and Mail*. Retrieved from http://www.theglobeandmail.com/report-on-business/careers/leadership-lab/how-to-navigate-your-career-with-intent/article31198562/

Victoria. (n.d.). A career plan. Retrieved from http://careers.vic.gov.au/exploration/a-fair-workplace

INDEX

J–K

L